31 Day Devotional

ELLA JONES

DEDICATION

To my Mother Gustava Barnett, the Woman that has Encouraged, Motivated and Inspired me to be my best me at all times. Not just by her words, but by being an example, her actions, her strength through all she has endured, and most of all her Faith in God. Much Love to my Mom.

I dedicate this devotional to the love of my life, Mr. Marcus L. Jones Sr. He has been my encouragement, inspiration and supporter from day one. I also dedicate it to the Mentees and Mentors of The Ruth and Naomi Youth Mentoring Program.

WORDS OF ENCOURAGEMENT

To say that I am proud of my wife for this devotional is an outright understatement. It has been amazing to watch her go from a woman still impeded by some insecurities from her childhood, to someone that is now allowing God to stretch her far beyond her comfort zone and use her to encourage others; particularly young ladies. I pray that God will allow this project to inspire, encourage, and empower young women to know their worth and embrace their true identity in Christ.

Sincerely,

A Proud Husband,

Minister Marcus L. Jones, Sr.

References

Holy Bible, NIV, NKJ

Webster dictionary

Bible study tools

www.wow4u.com

wikipedia

www.pintrest.com

Contents

KNOW YOUR WORTH

To know your worth is to know that you are just as good as anyone you interact with. We cannot think of being acceptable to others until we have first proven acceptable to ourselves. (Malcolm X)

It goes beyond admiring what is great and marvelous, but acknowledging in a public manner what is good and entitled to honor and love.

Psalm 139:14, I will praise thee: for I am Fearfully and Wonderfully made: marvelous are thy works: and that my soul knoweth right well.

STOP GIVING OUT DISCOUNTS ON YOUR LIFE

HAVE A PLAN

Habakkuk 2:2, Write the vision: make it plain on tablets, so he may easily run to read it.

Know what it takes to do what it is you desire.

Where do you start?   What is required?

Estimated time of action?   Financial set up? Etc...

Get all the details.

Jeremiah 29:11, for I know the plans I have for you and not to harm you, plans to give you hope and a future.

GOOD NEWS: Prov 16:3 Commit to the Lord whatever you do, and He will establish your plans.

YOU ARE VALUABLE

Your value does not decrease based on someone's inability to see your worth.

Isaiah 60:1... Arise, shine, for your light has come, and the glory of the Lord rises upon you.

The presence of the Lord is shining upon you. You are full of light and prosperity. Our hope is in God's ability to remove our fractured world and bring reconciliation.

Proverbs 3:15... She is more precious than rubies; nothing you desire can compare with her.

VALUE YOU

DAILY PRAYER

Prayer is the means by which we approach God, its deliberate communication. We are to talk to Him daily to build a relationship and get to know him better so we will know His voice.

Matthew 6:9-13... Our father, which art in heaven, hallowed be thy name, thy kingdom come, thy will be done in earth, as it is in heaven. Give us this day our daily bread and forgive us our trespass against us. Lead us not into temptation but deliver us from evil. For thine is the kingdom, the power and the glory, forever and ever. Amen

Prayer of Adoration

Prayer of Forgiveness

Prayer of Need

Prayer of Gratitude

PRAY CONSTANTLY

DAILY AFFIRMATION

Each day, take the time to speak positive words to yourself. Give yourself permission to be you. Learn to love yourself and believe in yourself. Make it a part of your daily life. Accept responsibility of yourself.

Romans 8:16... We are God's children. The spirit Himself testifies with our spirit that we are God's children.

Once we get that truth in our heart, spirit, we will love ourselves better, give ourselves dily affirmation...

I am Enough as I am

NEW CREATION

When we make the decision to walk in newness, we will no longer live like the world. We have a new birth brought about by the will of God, not re-created by ourselves, but by God's will. Old things are gone away, old habits, former opinions, past actions, etc... Dead things replaced with new, we see the word differently, new wonders. Renewed

II Corinthians 5:17... Therefore, if anyone is in Christ, he is a new creation. The old has passed away; behold, the new has come.

NEW EXISTENCE IN THE IMAGE OF GOD

DISCIPLINE

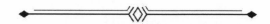

Obedience, self control,

a matter of rules, code of behavior

Discipline is defined as a punishment of unfavorable behavior and correction.

II Tim 1:7... For the spirit God gave us does not make us timid, but gives us power, love and self-discipline.

Discipline helps to achieve success in life by obeying the rules or standards of behaviour and the punishment that comes along when not met. Discipline brings stability and structure into a person's life.

Proverbs 12:1... Whoever loves discipline loves knowledge, but whoever hates correction is stupid.

The more disciplined you become, the easier life gets.

VISION

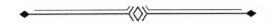

Have a vision, a purpose, and a plan. We are a part of the puzzle that moves the vision forward.

Vision is the act or power of sensing with the eyes; sight

Habakkuk 2:2... The LORD answered me: Write the vision, make it plain on tablets, so he may run that readeth it.

A vision defines what you aspire to become. Affirmations that help us discoverour true desires. A clear vision, partnered with courage to carry it out, increases your chance of success.

Make it plain, easy to understand.

GO GET IT

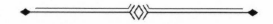

Eliminate distractions; elevate your determination, eraticate doubt.

Do Not Move From Your Goal

Time Out For Waiting, Go For It.

Acts 26:16... But get up and stand on your feet; for this purpose I have appeared to you, to appoint you a minister and a witness not only to the things which you have seen, but also to the things in which I will appear to you.

IT'S YOUR TIME

BE GRATEFUL

Show appreciation of kindness; be thankful. Express gratitude.

Always give thanks because God has been good to us. His mercy is never-ending. Each day He extends fresh grace to us for that I'm grateful.

Psalm 107:1... Oh give thanks to the Lord, for He is good, for His steadfast love endures forever.

Thank You

POSITIVE THINKING

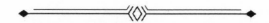

To be positive, is to be optimistic, confident, have good qualities, and be hopeful.

Have a good attitude that sees the good and the accomplichments in your life, rather than focusing on the negative things in life. Remove anything that brings negativity. Get rid of things that serve no purpose, do not dwell on the past.

Deuteronomy 31:6... Be strong and courageous. Do not fear or be in dread of them, for it is the Lord your God who goes with you. He will not leave you or forsake you.

Positive Mind. Positive Vibes. Positive Life.

FIND YOU

Knowing yourself is the beginning of all wisdom.

Believe in you and your own brand. Represent yourself well.

Don't be what others want you to be, be who God called you to be. Be a carbon-copy of things that has no identity.

Ephesians 2:10... For we are God's handiwork, created in Christ Jesus to do good works, which God prepared in advance for us to do.

Know your limits without limiting yourself.

UNITY

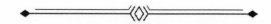

The state of being united or joined together

God calls His people to live in unity with one another, it's important to live together in harmony with other fellow believers. We should live in harmony with one another, in accord with Christ Jesus.

John 17:23... I in them and you in me so that they may be brought to complete unity. Then the world will know that you sent me and have loved them even as you have loved me...

We are only as strong as we are united. As weak as we are divided

EXPECTATION

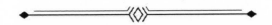

Having an expectation is a strong belief that something will happen.

Hope is a feeling of expectation and desire for a certain thing to happen. Look for, expect, and make the Lord the object of your Hope and Trust, expecting all good things from Him.

Seek God in the wait, the waiting is necessary

Psalm 39:7... And now, Lord, what do I wait for and expect? My hope and expectation are in you.

Walk In Expectancy

TRUTH

The truth is a fact or belief that is accepted at true.

There's a gap between our truth (as we know it) and the person we show the world, keep it 100. Always be who you are. Know the truth of God, study His word for yourself.

Know your truth, have the facts without allowing other's to speak what they dictate as the truth. Your truth is rooted in your belief.

1Kings 17:24... Then the woman said to Elijah, now I know you are a Man of God and that the word of the Lord from your mouth is the truth.

What Is Your Truth?

FOCUS

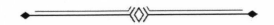

Staying focused is important to our thinking, memory, perception, learning, reasoning, decision making, and problem solving, it brings Clarity.

Be the center of your interest, and adjust to your well being. Have clear direction of where you're going; place your attention on your destination.

Colossians 3:2... Set your affection on things above, not on things on the earth.

Give attention to the task at hand

HAPPINESS -vs- JOY

Happiness is a pleasant emotion of contentment, satisfaction, and well- being, based on (something good happening)

Psalm 37:4... Delight yourself in the Lord, and He will give you the desires of your heart.

Joy is settled assurance that God is in control, the Joy of the Lord is our strength, Neh 8:10.

Romans 12:12... Be joyful in hope patient in affliction, faithful in prayer.

This joy I have, the world didn't give it, and the world can't take it away

COMMUNICATION

James 1:19... Know this, my beloved brothers, let every person be quick to hear, slow to speak, slow to anger.

Communication is exchanging information, sharing ideas, and listening. We can reach a better understanding of another by talking out feelings, truth, and facts.

Ephesians 4:29... Let no corrupting talk come out of your mouths, but only such as is good for building up, as fits the occasion, that it may give grace to those who hear.

TALK ABOUT IT.

You Are An OVERCOMER

An overcomer is a person that succeeds in dealing with or gaining control of some problem of difficulty. As an Overcomer we walk by faith not by sight Corinthians 5:7. The Lord is our strength and shield, in Him our heart trusts, and we are helped Psalm 28:7.

The Lord is our light and salvation: whom shall I fear Psalm 27:1.

I have said these things to you, that in me you may have peace. In the world you will have tribulation. But take heart; I have overcome the world. John 16:3

Conquer, and remain steadfast through trials.

You Are Qualified

To be qualified is the ability to perform, experienced, trained.

Romans 8:30... And those He predestined, He also called; those He called, He also justified, those He justified, He also glorified.

Those God called, He equips.

2 Corinthians 3:5, Not that we are competent in ourselves to claim anything for ourselves, but our competence comes from God.

We can't do it ourselves, but when God calls us to it, He qualifies us for it.

Through Him we're fit for the task.

Options & Decisions

Options are a thing that is or may be chosen, Decisions are the conclusion or resolution reached after consideration.

Proverbs 2:6, for the God gives wisdom; from His mouth come knowledge and understanding.

Choose Gods Plan

When making choices and decisions, trust in the Lord with all your heart and do not lean not unto thine own understanding. In all thy ways acknowledge Him, and He shall direct thy paths Prov 3:5-6

When someone treats you like an option, help them narrow their choices by removing yourself from the equation, it's that simple.

GROWTH

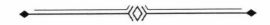

In our growth process, we blossom, develop, and mature. We do things differently, we react to situations in a different manner, we are careful about how we respond to life.

2 Peter 3:18, But grow in the grace and knowledge of our Lord and savior Jesus Christ. To Him be glory both now and forever.

Job 8:7, And though your beginning was small, your latter days will be great.

Be not afraid of growing slowly; be afraid only of standing stll

PRIDE

Pride can be defined as deep pleasure or satisfaction of our own achievements, confidence, and self respect. It can be used in a good sense as well as a bad sense. We cannot think to highly of ourselves, although we are not better than others, we are just as good.

Proverbs 8:13, To fear the Lord is to hate evil; I hate Pride and arrogance, evil behavior and perverse speech.

Types of Pride: Dignity, Superiority and Arrogance.

INSPIRATION

Being inspired is to be mentally stimulated to do or feel something, getting a feeling of enthusiasm from someone of something which gives you a new and creative idea.

Excite, Encourage or Breathe life into

2 Tim 3:16, tells us that all Scripture is inspired by God and useful for teaching, rebuking, correcting and training in righteousness.

The word of God is my biggest inspiration.

LEADER

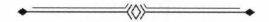

To be a Leader you must have morals and ethical courage, set an example, and have open communication. Along with it, there's honesty, confidence, committment, determination, positive attitude, creativity, and discipline.

Jeremiah 1:5, Before I formed you in the womb I knew you, before you were born I set you apart; I appointed you as a prophet to the nations.

God set us in position before we were.

He formed us for particular services and purposes; we are to lead in our purpose

A good leader has been, and is still, a good follower of truth.

FAITH

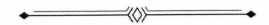

HEBREWS 11:1, Now Faith is the substance of things hoped for, the evidence of things not seen. (Walking by Faith)

Faith is to have a strong belief in God or in the doctrines of a religion, based on spiritual apprehension rather than proof. It's to have complete trust or confidence in someone or something.

Faith is just as important as the air we breathe.

LOVE

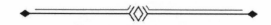

Webster defines Love as an intense feeling of deep affection. However,

A deeper meaning of Love from the word of God explains it all: Love is patient, Love is kind, Does not envy, Is not proud, Does not dishonor others, Not self seeking, Not easily angered, Keeps no record of wrongs.

Types of Love: Eros= Romantic

Storage=Empathy

Philia= Friend

Agape= Unconditional

Gods Love is our example of how to love others.

RESPECT

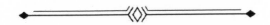

To have respect for someone is to admire deeply, as a result of ability, qualities, or achievements. It's a way of treating or thinking of someone, respect is shown by being polite and kind.

Characteristics consist of being patient, considerate, dealing with peacefully without anger, insults and disagreements. Also includes showing gratitude, compliment achievements, and keeping your word.

1st Peter 2:17, Show proper respect to everyone, love the family of believers, fear God, and honor the emperor.

Give Respect Receive Respect

UNIQUELY YOU

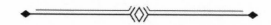

What sets you apart is what makes you great.

No need to feel required to fit into someone else's definition of who you should be. It's okay to be uniquely you.

It's great to be the indivual you were created to be, an original, not an copy.

You Are A Masterpiece Created By The Master.

BE BOLD

To be bold is to show an ability to take risks; confident and courageous.

The doors will be open to those bold enough to knock. Be bold enough to use your voice, brave enough to listen to your heart and strong enough to live the life you've always imagined.

Hebrews 4:16, Let us therefore come boldly to the throne of grace, that we may obtain mercy and find grace in time of need.

Be bold, Be Brave. Be Courageous

VICTORIOUS

Triumphant, Victory, Conqueror

We have been given authority over every trick of the enemy; our Heavenly Father paid a heavy price to make us Victorious.

Deuteronomy 20:4, For the Lord your God is the one who goes with you to fight for you against yoir enemies to give you Victory.

Walk In Your Victory!

Made in the USA
Middletown, DE
23 March 2020